GET A JOB AT THE SHOPPING MALL

DIANE LINDSEY REEVES

Created and produced by
Bright Futures Press, Cary, North Carolina
www.brightfuturespress.com

Published by
Cherry Lake Publishing, Ann Arbor, Michigan
www.cherrylakepublishing.com

Photo Credits: cover, Shutterstock/Kzenon; page 4, Shutterstock/YIUCHEUNG; page 5, Shutterstock/ISO100; page 7, Shutterstock/Diego Cervo; page 7, Shutterstock/Zhukov Oleg; page 9, Shutterstock/zhv d. feng; page 11, Shutterstock/Africa Studio; page 11, Shutterstock/Faraways; page 13, Shutterstock/Pavel L Photo and Video; page 15, Shutterstock/Catwalk Photos; page 15, Shutterstock/wavebreakmedia; page 17, Shutterstock/Sylvie Bouchard; page 17, Shutterstock/jassada watt; page 19, Shutterstock/bikeriderlondon; page 21, Shutterstock/5 second Studio; page 23, Shutterstock/GavdiLab; page 23, Shutterstock/Kenishirotie; page 25, Shutterstock/Anton Gvozdikov; page 26, Shutterstock/Monkey Business Images; page 27, Shutterstock/Iakov Filimonor; page 28, Shutterstock/Robert Kneshke.

Illustrated by Chris Griffin

Library of Congress Cataloging-in-Publication Date

CIP data has been filed and is available at catalog.loc.gov.

Printed in the United States of America

TABLE OF CONTENTS

Ready to shop till you drop?

If so, you are not alone. In the U.S. alone, there are about 20 million kids, affectionately known as tweens, between the ages of 8 and 12. Experts say that, all told, billions of dollars are spent by or on tweens every year. Lots of this money finds its way to local **retail** stores. That's where tweens buy clothes, entertainment, and technology.

It's time for back-to-school shopping, and a fictional kid named **J**eremiah **O**liver **B**aumgartner heads to the local mall with his mom. The kid's initials are J.O.B., so his friends call him Job for short. His parents like his nickname because sometimes it is hard work parenting a kid like Job. It's not that Job is a troublemaker. He's a great kid. But trouble seems to go out of its way to find him.

Job expects a fun day playing arcade games while his mom shops for his new school wardrobe. But Job's mom has other plans for the day. She's about to turn him loose on his very first shopping spree, while she enjoys a day of leisure at the **spa**.

Tag along with Job as he gains a new understanding of the saying "shop till you drop." As he explores the mall, you can explore the different jobs people do to fill all those stores with products you want to buy.

SHOPPING BIT

Retail accounts for one in four American jobs. Retail (and all the jobs it supports) adds $2.6 trillion to the U.S. economy.

CHAPTER I
JOB GOES TO THE MALL

Job and his mom were at the mall. It was time for back-to-school shopping.

Job's mom usually did the shopping while he goofed off. This year Job was in for a surprise.

"Now that you're older and sort of mature," Job's mom began.

"Yes! I can go to the arcade all by myself?" Job interrupted. With thirty bucks of birthday money in his pocket, he could play games all day!

"Uh, not exactly," Mom said. "Here's a shopping list and a cell phone. Call me when it is time to pay."

"Huh?" Job stared at the long list. "You want me to pick out my own clothes this year?"

"Call my cell phone when you are ready and I'll come pay," his mom explained.

"Wait ..." Job started to complain, but his mom had already headed into the nearby spa. It was her turn to goof off.

Every product you see starts with an idea. **Product designers** take ideas and turn them into products. They start by asking lots of questions, and the answers to these questions guide the design process. What need does this product fill? How will it be used? What are the best materials to use? Product designers develop **prototypes** to test and refine concepts before sending products into production.

Fashion designers start fashion trends.

Every item on display in your favorite store was designed by a **fashion designer**. This includes clothes, accessories, shoes, and even undergarments. Fashion designers sketch out ideas, select fabrics, and provide instructions on how to make their creations. They keep up with the latest **trends**, and the best designers create new trends featured in glossy magazines and glamorous places like Paris and New York City.

Clothes are made by putting pieces of fabric together in specific ways, like a puzzle to fit people of different sizes. **Patternmakers** use sketches made by fashion designers to create patterns for constructing garments. It takes creative flair and solid math skills to accurately measure the sections that make up garments, like sleeves or collars. Patterns provide precise guides for making the millionth shirt look exactly like the first.

Tools of the fashion trade.

SHOPPING BIT

Consumers in the United States buy approximately 450 million pairs of blue jeans every year.

Let's say a clothing manufacturer gets a big order for jeans. In order to make the jeans, the manufacturer needs denim fabric, special dyes, thread, sturdy zippers, and snaps. A **director of sourcing** finds the needed materials at a fair price from reliable **vendors**. A big part of this job is getting the materials where they need to be on time.

A manufacturer takes the ideas, the designs, the patterns, and all the materials and turns them into products. Manufacturers work in factories or plants full of high-tech equipment. These machines **automate** the production process and make it possible to produce large quantities of products quickly.

THE RESULTS

Job decided to get the shopping over with. That way he'd still have plenty of time for the arcade.

"How hard can it be to find some jeans and T-shirts?" Job asked himself.

He spotted the information booth right away, and next to it the neon-lit map of the mall. There were dozens of stores listed on it!

"Hmmm …" Job said. "I wonder where the cool kids shop?"

CHAPTER 2

JOB GOES ON A SHOPPING SPREE

Job headed to his mom's favorite department store first.

He took the escalator upstairs. He passed through baby clothes and toys, the girls' section, and ladies lingerie. Ew! Job kept his eyes on the floor and walked really fast past that department

Finally, he was in the guys' junior department. "Wow! Look at all this stuff!"

He looked at the top of his shopping list: three pairs of blue jeans. "No problem," he thought.

Job found where the jeans were displayed. There were racks and racks full of jeans! There were dark blue jeans and light blue jeans. Some jeans looked like they'd already been worn for a hundred years with holes in the knees and other places. Then Job turned a corner and found another wall of Levis™, and that's when Job broke into a cold sweat.

Job's mom made it look so easy. Now here he was, on his own, with all these choices. "I want my mama!" he moaned.

Fashion buyers shop for a living. Buyers shop for entire departments or stores, looking for the best merchandise for consumers to purchase. They travel, attend **trade shows**, talk with fashion consultants, meet with sales

representatives, and keep in touch with customers. Fashion buyers analyze which fashions to buy, and how many of each item to stock.

A **fashion importer** is someone who brings in clothing made in foreign countries for sale or trade. Fashion importers are the **liaison**, or connection, between a foreign company that makes clothing to export and a local business that wants to import clothing to sell. Fashion importers handle the many details that make this possible—including doing lots of paperwork!

Fashion buyers fill stores with the latest fashions.

Getting clothes from the places where they are made to the places where they are sold is what a **global logistics manager** does. This process often begins by arranging to ship huge containers full of clothing from **manufacturers** around the world. Once these ships arrive at their intended ports, products are shipped by trucks and by railroad to warehouses. From there, products are distributed to individual stores. This is all part of what is called the **supply chain**.

Imagine a huge empty room about the size of a football field. Add row after row

Some clothes travel a long way to get to local malls.

SHOPPING BIT

There are nearly 47,000 shopping centers in the United States. Only about 1,100 are enclosed malls.

of huge shelves, plus a fleet of lifts and conveyors used to move heavy merchandise. Now, in your mind, fill those shelves with big boxes of Nike™ shoes and other sports gear. Enter the **warehouse manager**. The warehouse manager is in charge of keeping track of all that inventory and getting it where it needs to go.

THE RESULTS

Job took a deep breath and tried to calm down. He looked around at all the people rushing by. Most of them looked like they were enjoying themselves. Maybe shopping on his own would be a good thing. He could go for a whole new look. What he needed was a plan!

"If only one of these stores sold shopping plans," Job sighed. Then he made a list of all the stores he wanted to visit.

CHAPTER 3

JOB MAKES A FASHION STATEMENT

“It’s time for our back-to-school fashion show,” came a voice over the store’s public-address system.

Job headed out to see the show but he ended up behind the stage. It was crowded, and there were a bunch of girls waiting in line. Then he bumped into a pretty lady holding a clipboard and wearing a headset.

“You’re on!” she loudly whispered into his ear, and gave Job a not-so-gentle push forward.

Job found himself standing onstage in front of a big crowd of cheering people. Job froze for a moment in the spotlight.

Then he waved at the crowd, took a bow, and walked to the end of the stage runway—making a beeline for the nearest exit.

Modeling is considered a glamorous career, and it can be. But modeling also requires long hours of hard work and talent. **Models** promote fashions in magazines, commercials, advertisements, and fashion shows. Looking good is their job!

Event planners plan fun events for stores, malls, or specific fashion brands. They choose the event location and take care of things like décor, music, food, and flowers. It takes a lot of work to stage a fun event!

Marketing managers figure out the best mix of activities to promote their clients' products. They create commercials and ads that promote products on television, in print, and online. Marketing managers look for ways to reach specific audiences that get the most bang from their budgets.

Models show off the latest fashions.

Commercial producers work with actors, camera operators, and sound engineers to produce commercials. These 30- to 60-second film clips target specific types of audiences; like the ads you see when watching your favorite shows.

Catalog copywriters write the words that describe the pictures you see in fashion catalogs. The challenge is to expertly match content and tone with the intended audience in as few words as possible.

Graphic designers are visual artists who make words and images look good in print. They design the attention-grabbing pages for catalogs, advertisements, and signs. They also design **logos** that give brands a distinct identity.

Graphic designers create sales catalogs.

THE RESULTS

Job got far away from the fashion show and parked himself on a bench. He watched as lots of kids his age went in and out of a nearby store. Many of the kids were loaded down with bags with the store's logo on it.

"Oh yeah," Job remembered. "This is the store with those funny commercials on TV."

Job looked at the mannequins on display in the store's windows. One of them was wearing a dark pair of blue jeans, a cool T-shirt, and awesome sneakers.

Job went inside the store and leaned into the display window for a better look at the shoes. Unfortunately, when Job tried to read the price tag he lost his balance and crashed—with a thud— into the mannequin.

Job was trying to untangle himself from the mess when someone behind him shouted, "Security!"

SHOPPING BIT

Retailers send out nearly 13 billion catalogs a year. That's about 35 catalogs for every man, woman, and child in the United States.

CHAPTER 4
JOB GETS A FASHION MAKEOVER

When Job's mom showed up at the store, Job knew he was in big trouble.

She had some kind of green goo all over her face, and she did not look happy. "What did you do now, Job?" she asked.

"It was an accident! I tripped!" Job said. "I wasn't trying to steal anything."

The loss prevention officer explained that the store manager thought that Job was trying to swipe the shoes off the mannequin. He apologized for the mistake and offered a 25 percent discount off the shoes Job liked to make up for it.

There's nothing Job's mom likes better than a discount. She bought not one, but two pairs of the shoes.

"Sweet," Job said, showing off the blue pair. "I should almost get arrested for not shoplifting more often."

Loss prevention officers work to stop shoplifting and theft from stores. They are part of the security team that sometimes includes the uniformed security officers who patrol stores in a more visible way. Loss prevention officers work behind the scenes and keep an eye on customers by watching video footage from hidden cameras. They may also develop plans for theft prevention and provide reports about how much inventory is lost to **shoplifters** and thieves.

Security guards keep an eye out for trouble.

One thing that **visual merchandisers** do is dress **mannequins** to display merchandise in store windows. But their job involves much more than dressing dummies. They also come up with eye-catching window displays, decorate stores for holidays, and make a visual splash for special promotions.

Sales associates help customers find what they need, ring up sales on the cash register, and bag merchandise. They also stock shelves and set up merchandise displays. Sales associates are often the only employees that customers encounter in a store. It is important that they are friendly, knowledgeable about the store's products, and helpful. Customer service is the number one priority of a sales associates everywhere!

Store managers are responsible for running the day-to-day business of a store. They are in charge of scheduling, paying, hiring (and firing) of all employees. Store managers keep track of the store's inventory, and they make sure that

May I help you?

SHOPPING BIT

Shoplifting and employee theft cost American retailers $32 billion a year.

products and signs are displayed properly.

Every retail store has its own way of doing things. When new employees are hired, a **trainer** teaches them how things are done. Good training helps employees develop and improve skills, shows them how to work in smarter ways, and makes them feel like a valued part of the company. Well-trained employees help stores attract and keep customers.

THE RESULTS

After the mannequin mess, Job wasn't sure how he was going to find the rest of the items on his list. He was wandering around another store when a cool-looking teen introduced himself. He was wearing a name tag and asked if Job needed any help.

"Do I ever!" Job exclaimed and showed the sales associate his list.

The sales associated helped Job figure out what sizes he wore and brought him lots of clothes to try on in the fitting room.

"This is almost as good as having Mom do the shopping for me," Job said.

CHAPTER 5
JOB SHOPS 'TIL HE DROPS

Many clothes-changes later, Job called his mom.

She showed up with a smile on her face (and no green goo!).

Mom went through the selections Job had made with a look of amazement on her face. "Who knew you had such good taste?" she said.

"Just call me super shopper dude," Job said proudly. He had survived his first shopping spree!

Then Job saw some of his classmates coming into the store. "On second thought, don't. It will be better if we never mention this day again."

If you know the brand name of some of your favorite clothes, it is because a **brand manager** did a good job. Brand managers are in charge of a specific product within a big company, like Legos™, Barbie™, or Levis™. Brand managers give each brand a distinct "personality" and oversee promotion and sales. They do lots of research to make sure their brand connects with the right customers, so people will keep buying their brand of products.

Many companies have multiple stores in more than one location. Some companies have stores all over the country, or even the world! **District managers** oversee the operations of stores in specific areas, or districts. They set budgets and make sure each store makes its sales goals. Travel is involved, because district managers visit each store to make sure it is clean, well-stocked, and projecting the right corporate image.

Merchandisers set up displays in stores.

A **merchandiser** comes up with plans to sell the merchandise that fashion buyers bring into stores each season. They come up with ideas for displaying the merchandise and share instructions on how to display specific products in certain ways. That way a customer can come into one of their stores in any location and encounter the same products in the same way.

Merchandise analysts keep track of inventory and make charts that show the profits and sales of each store or an entire company. It's the merchandise analyst's job to notice consumer patterns and to alert store managers, buyers, and other corporate decision makers when products sell exceptionally well or when they flop. All this data helps stores know when it's time

Analysts keep track of inventory and sales.

SHOPPING BIT

The day after Christmas, December 26, is the best day to find bargains on clothes.

to order more of the "hot" products and when to put slow-moving products on sale.

Like other big companies, retail corporations have lots of support staff who help keep the business running smoothly, like people in administration, credit card services, accounting, and purchasing. There are also people who work in corporate communications, government affairs, human resources, and legal services. Bottom line, it takes lots of people with lots of different kinds of skills to keep people looking good and dressed for success!

THE RESULTS

After they checked out, Mom said, "One more stop." She guided Job down the hall. He was too tired to complain.

"Surprise!" she said. "I'm ready for some fun and games at the arcade after a relaxing day at the spa. How about you, Job?"

Job didn't answer. He'd already found his favorite game and conked out. It had been an exhausting day!

"I guess this is what it means to shop till you drop," Job's mom said with a smile.

CHAPTER 6

WHO DOES WHAT AT SHOPPING MALLS?

WHO DOES WHAT?

Job met some interesting people during his trip to the shopping mall. Can you match their job titles with the correct job descriptions?

Please do NOT write in this book if it is not yours. Use a separate piece of paper.

1. The pretty woman who nudged Job onto the stage during the fashion show
2. The man who talked to Job's mom about the mannequin incident
3. The helpful teen who helped Job find a nice selection of back-to-school clothes
4. The person who set up the mannequins and other visual displays that caught Job's eye
5. The person who designed the logo that Job recognized on the shopping bags

A. Visual merchandiser

B. Graphic designer

C. Loss prevention officer

D. Sales associate

E. Event planner

Answer Key: 1-E; 2-C; 3-D; 4-A; 5-B

WHO? WHAT? WHERE?

Choose the correct job description to complete the sentences below:

1. _____ turn ideas into products that can be sold.
2. _____ keep track of how much merchandise is sold in stores.
3. A fashion _____ models clothes in catalogs and fashion shows.
4. _____ shop for a living.
5. _____ teach new employees how things are done in a store.

A. Fashion buyers
B. Model
C. Product designers
D. Trainers
E. Merchandise analysts

Answer key: 1-C; 2-E; 3-B; 4-A; 5-D

CHAPTER 7
IT'S YOUR TURN

Shopping proved to be quite the adventure for Job.

Share a shopping adventure that you or a family member had. Be sure to mention all the people who helped you along the way.

Go online to download a free activity sheet at **www.cherrylakepublishing.com/activities**.

GLOSSARY

automate
to run or operate something using machines instead of people

brand manager
person in charge of promoting a specific product within a company

catalog copywriter
person who writes words to accompany photographs shown in product catalogs

commercial producer
person who films product advertisements to be broadcast on radio, television, or online

director of sourcing
person who finds and gathers all the materials needed to make a product

district manager
person who oversees the operations of several stores in a specific region

event planner
person who organizes promotional events for businesses or stores

fashion buyer
person who chooses what fashion items their stores will carry each season

fashion designer
person who designs clothing or fashion accessories

fashion importer
person who brings in products from foreign countries to sell

global logistics manager
person who finds and gathers all the materials needed to produce a product

graphic designer
person who designs pages for catalogs, advertisements, signs, and other materials used to promote businesses

liaison
a person who helps organizations or groups to work together and provide information to each other

logos
symbols or other designs adopted by organizations to identify their products

loss prevention officer
person who works to prevent shoplifting and theft in stores and businesses

mannequin
a dummy used to display clothes in a store window

manufacturer
a company that runs a factory or plant that mass-produces products for consumers

marketing manager
person who plans promotional ideas for a product or brand

merchandise analyst
person who keeps track of how much product is selling in a specific store or company

merchandiser
person who makes plans to sell specific merchandise in a store

model
person who wears clothes for promotion in catalogs, fashion shows, and other media

patternmaker
person who creates patterns for making a specific garment

product designer
person who creates new products to be sold by a business to its customers

prototypes
early samples or models of products

retail
the sale of goods to the public for personal consumption

sales associate
person who assists customers in making purchases at a store

shoplifter
person who steals goods from the shelves or displays of a retail store while posing as a customer

spa
a store offering health and beauty treatments

store manager
person who runs the day-to-day operations of a store

supply chain
the processes involved in producing and distributing a product

trade show
a large gathering where different companies in a particular field or industry show their products to possible customers

trainer
person who teaches employees how to conduct business at a store

trends
general directions in which fashion is developing or changing

vendor
a person or company offering something for sale

visual merchandiser
person who creates displays for store windows and other retail promotions

warehouse manager
person in charge of all the inventory that moves into and out of a warehouse

INDEX

ABOUT THE AUTHOR

Diane Lindsey Reeves is the author of lots of children's books. She has written several original PEANUTS stories (published by Regnery Kids and Sourcebooks). She is especially curious about what people do and likes to write books that get kids thinking about all the cool things they can be when they grow up. She lives in Cary, North Carolina, and her favorite thing to do is play with her grandkids—Conrad, Evan, Reid, and Hollis Grace.